D1271696

DATE DUE

SEP 1 7 2003	
10-16	
Feb 9	

DEMCO, INC. 38-2931

People of the Middle Ages
Peasant

Melinda Lilly

Original illustrations by Cheryl Goettemoeller

Rourke

Publishing LLC
Vero Beach, Florida 32964

www.rourkepublishing.com

For Joyce

To My Darling Daughters, Laurena and Jade - C.G.

PICTURE CREDITS: Page 5, "The Annunciation to the Shepherds," from a *Book of Hours, Llangattock Hours,* unknown, about 1450–1460, 26.4 x 18.4 cm., The J. Paul Getty Museum, Los Angeles; Page 6, "A Man and a Woman Reaping: Zodiacal Sign of Leo," from a Book of Hours, Workshop of the Bedford Master, about 1440–1450, 23.5 x 16 cm., The J. Paul Getty Museum, Los Angeles; Page 14, top, page detail of "Initial C: The Massacre of the Innocents," from a *Breviary,* unknown, about 1320–1325, 16.6 x 11.1 cm., The J. Paul Getty Museum, Los Angeles; Page 14, bottom, page detail of "Initial O: The Massacre of the Innocents," from a *Breviary,* unknown, about 1320–1325, 16.6 x 11.1 cm., The J. Paul Getty Museum, Los Angeles; Page 17, page detail of "Initial Q: A Woman with Bread Loaves Before a Man Holding a Scale," from the *Vidal Mayor,* possibly Michael Lupi de Çandiu (illuminator and scribe), about 1290–1310, 36.5 x 24 cm., The J. Paul Getty Museum, Los Angeles; Page 18, MS. Douce 346, fol. 183, courtesy of the Bodleian Library, University of Oxford; Original art on the cover and pages 9, 10, 13, 21, 22, 25, 26, and 29 is by Cheryl Goettemoeller.

Cover illustration: Oxen were used in the Middle Ages (years 500 to 1500) to pull plows.

Editor: Frank Sloan

Cover design by Nicola Stratford

Library of Congress Cataloging-in-Publication Data

Lilly, Melinda
    Peasant / Melinda Lilly
     p. cm. — (People of the Middle Ages)
    Includes bibliographical references and index.
    Summary: An introduction to the work and social life of peasants in Europe in the Middle Ages.
    ISBN 1-58952-229-X
    1.Peasantry—Europe—History—Juvenile literature. 2. Rural children—Europe—History—Juvenile literature. 3. Europe—Social conditions—To 1492—Juvenile literature. 4. Europe—Economic conditions—To 1492—Juvenile literature. 5. Peasantry—History—Juvenile literature. 6. Middle Ages—Juvenile literature. [1. Peasantry. 2. Middle Ages. 3. Civilization, Medieval.] I. Title. II. Series.

HD1531.5 .L55 2002   2001056509
305'633'0940902—dc21

Printed in the USA

CG/CG

Table of Contents

Welcome to the Middle Ages

"Waah!" you cry. You have just been born. Although your parents may not know the year, it is 1225. You live in Europe. What does your future hold? Chances are that you will be a peasant farmer. Nine out of ten people in the **Middle Ages** (the years 500 to 1500) are peasants.

You probably will not own the land you farm. Most landowners are the Church and **nobles**: royalty, lords, ladies, and knights.

Peasants dance to a bagpipe's music while guarding the castle's sheep.

A Peasant's Work Is Never Done

Cut that wheat! Milk that cow! Your job as a peasant is to provide food. You grow food for your family and for other people. Your harvest feeds nobles and people of the Church.

What do they do for you? Nobles are supposed to protect you. Priests and nuns pray for you. If they own your land, they are your bosses. Work, work, work!

Peasants harvest grain in this picture from a book of the 1400s.

There's No Place Like Home

Welcome home. Follow the goat through the open door and take a look around. There's one big room where you and your family live, and a penned area where the cow sleeps. Watch your step, it's dark and smoky inside, and a fire smolders in the middle of the dirt floor.

Your supper simmers in a pot over the fire. Sit down at the big wooden table and get ready for a meal of **porridge**, bread, and berries. Yum!

A peasant family prepares to eat.

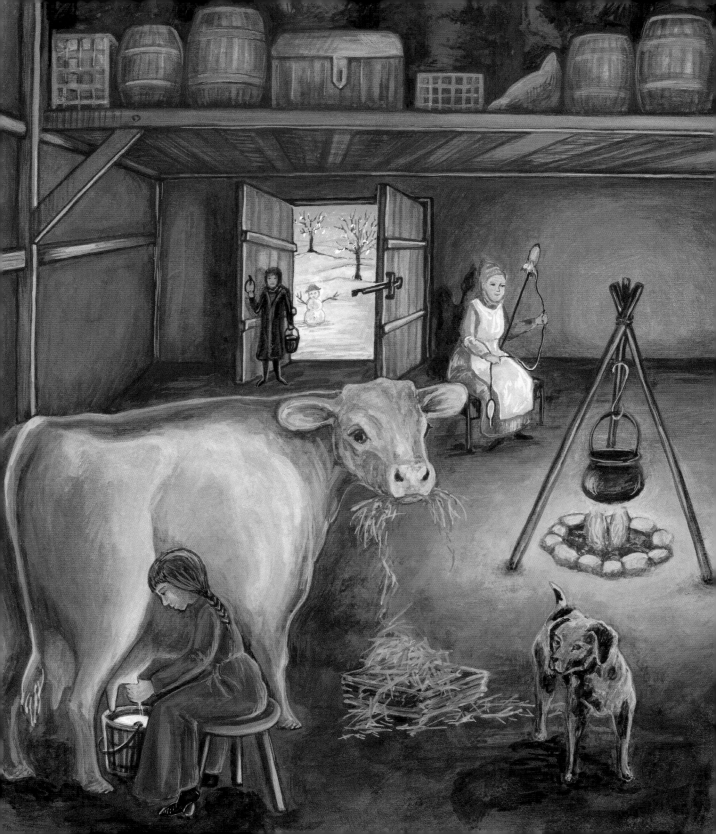

Women's Work

Get out of bed, sleepy-headed peasant girl!
Time to milk the cow. After a breakfast of
bread and milk, you spend the day helping
your mother. Baby-sit your younger sisters
and keep them out of trouble.

Have a moment? Hurry to the well for
water. Feed the chickens and geese. Clean the
wool before your mother spins it into thread.
Weed the fields. Pick berries and gather
firewood. Help make supper. Collapse into
bed and fall asleep.

A peasant girl and her mother work in their cottage.

11

Men's Work

"Come on, son." The chilly fall morning makes you shiver as you, your brother, and father lead the landlord's pigs down the path. At the oak trees, your father knocks down acorns to feed the pigs. You and your brother use a net to catch fish.

What about school? It's not for peasants. You learn only enough about numbers to help you buy and sell. Reading is the priest's job, not yours. He'll tell you what he thinks you should know.

Brothers fish while their father feeds acorns to the pigs.

Children play a ball game of the Middle Ages.

Children clap as one boy carries another piggy-back style.

Time to Play!

Chores are done! You have the rest of the day to play. Snow fell last night and ice is on the pond. Put a horse's shinbone on the bottom of each shoe. Grab a pole to help you balance and go ice skating!

How about a game of marbles, horseshoes, or bowling? Your brother tugs at your sleeve. He wants a piggyback ride. See how fast you can run while he giggles at your back!

15

To Market, to Market

Put a bag on your back and load it with vegetables, fresh bread, and cheese. You may look like a pack donkey, but it's worth it. If you enter the weekly market carrying your wares, you won't have to pay taxes on them.

Set up the stall that you've rented from the local landlord. "Fresh bread for sale!" you cry. Later you'll eat take-out food and chat with friends. Market day is work and fun!

A shopkeeper sells her bread after it is weighed. This picture is from a handmade book of the Middle Ages.

r ones
auiere
officiale͠s
te aueu
se aue
re men
ester fu

eren otre officio. o de quoal se
auiere digmidat en cara quo
anto fueren a pesar el pan te
uenter o fueren imbiados en
la casa o torno fuere o panes
fueren non deuen entrar por
razon te pesar panes. Enpo
los panes que son tendo en
la casa eucs seriento ante la
finiestra. o ante los umbra
res tela puerta cabo la casa

Holiday!

Hussa! It's January fifth, the feast of Twelfth Night. Toast your friends and take a bite of cake. You bite into a bean. Lucky you! The two people with beans in their cake are the king and queen of the party.

Sit on your "pretend" throne and watch dancers dressed as oxen. Lead your friends in a toast to the oldest tree in the neighborhood. At midnight, you'll watch a show about the Biblical three kings. Good night, royal bean!

*People in costume (called **mummers**) toss eggs as they travel to a holiday feast.*

Serf or Free

Not all peasants are the same. As a **serf**, you work your landlord's farm. Your landlord can decide where you live, which laws you must obey, even who you marry. However, you can own a business or land of your own as long as it does not interfere with your duties.

If you are free, you can own land or pay rent. You still work for the noble, but not as often as a serf. You can live as you wish.

Serfs work the noble's land.

Becoming a Serf

Why become a serf? Most free people do not become serfs unless they are very poor. However, if your parents are serfs, you will be a serf on the same land.

Serf, you must promise to serve your landlord. Kneel and clasp your hands. Your landlord's hands rest on yours. Promise to be loyal. Swear to it by placing your hand on a Bible. Your landlord kisses you to seal the agreement.

A man promises to serve his landlord.

A Serf's Life

You work on your landlord's farm three days each week. Don't take home any of the harvest! Your landlord owns everything grown on that land. You also owe taxes. Load up your cart with eighteen bundles of oats and a big basket filled with wheat. Deliver them and then pay your landlord three hens, a rooster, and five eggs.

You work hard. However, there are many holidays. Peasants of the Middle Ages worked fewer days than most adults of today.

Peasants harvest grain.

Milling Around

After taxes, you have grain left over for your food. Put it in a sack and carry it to the mill. You pay the owner of the mill—often your landlord—with some of the flour he grinds for you. Still, it's better than grinding flour by hand.

A **water mill** and a **windmill** are two important machines of the Middle Ages. A water mill uses water power to grind grain or do other tasks. A windmill uses wind to power its machinery.

Peasant women tote their grain to the water mill.

Freedom!

You don't want to be a serf anymore? Make a deal with your landlord to buy your freedom. When you're ready, meet your landlord in your cottage. After paying her price, she walks you out your door. When she closes it behind you, you're free!

What if you can't buy your freedom? You will have to escape. Run away to a town. Find work as a servant. After living inside town walls for one year, you are free!

An escaped serf works as a servant in town.

Dates to Remember

400s	Heavy plow in use in Northern Europe
476	Last Roman emperor overthrown (Romulus Augustulus)
500	Beginning of the Middle Ages
1100s	Hard soap is used in Europe (invented in the Middle East)
about 1185	Windmill (post mill) invented in England
1200s	Wheelbarrow used in Europe (used in China in the 200s)
1200s	Spinning wheel brought to Europe from India
1215	Magna Carta issued; this document limits the power of English royalty
1500	End of the Middle Ages

Glossary

hussa (huh ZAH) — Hooray, as said by people in the Middle Ages

Middle Ages (MID ul AY jez) — a time in European history that lasted from the year 500 to 1500

mummers (MUM urz) — people who wear costumes or masks as part of a show or festival

nobles (NO bulz) — people of high social class

porridge (POR idj) — a food made of cereal cooked in water or milk

serf (SURF) — a person who must serve the owner of a farm on which he or she works

water mill (WAH ter MIL) — a machine powered by rushing water

windmill (WIND mil) — a machine powered by the force of wind pushing upon sails or blades

Index

Further Reading

Chrisp, Peter. *The Middle Ages.* Two-Can Publishers, 2000.
Langley, Andrew. *Eyewitness: Medieval Life*. DK Publishing, 2000.
MacDonald, Fiona. *Women in Medieval Times.* NTC/ContemporaryPublishing Company, 2000.

Websites to Visit

The life of a serf
www.geocities.com/Athens/Bridge/4328/
Overview of the Middle Ages
http://people.clemson.edu/~elizab/medievalgallery.htm

About the Author

Melinda Lilly is the author of several children's books. Some of her past jobs have included editing children's books, teaching preschool, and working as a reporter for *Time* magazine. She is the author of *Around The World With Food & Spices* also from Rourke.